Food for the Soul

A
"Best of *Bereavement*"
poetry collection

Edited by
ANDREA GAMBILL

Foreword by
Alan D. Wolfelt, Ph. D.

Bereavement Publishing, Inc.
Colorado Springs, Colorado

Bereavement Publishing, Inc.
5125 N. Union Boulevard, Suite 4
Colorado Springs, CO 80918

Editor: Andrea Gambill
Art Direction/Visual Design: Tom Myers
Cover Design: Tom Myers • Calligraphy: Jane Myers

Artwork pgs. 5, 17, 20, 65 and photography pgs. 21, 28-30, 34, 36, 58 —
© 1996 Tom Myers. All rights reserved.

Poetry by Joanetta Hendel reprinted with permission from
God Will Teach me to Fly ©1996, Word Works Publishing

Contents

Foreword

By Alan D. Wolfelt, Ph.D.

While sometimes words are inadequate in the face of grief, at other times language — in all its various forms — can be extremely healing for the bereaved. Poetry in particular seems to hold healing powers. Its rhythm soothes; its brevity condenses a universe of insight into just a few words. Writer and reader alike learn and grow from their encounters with this centuries-old form of expression.

I have been privileged to meet thousands of grieving people in my twenty years as a grief counselor and educator. Over and over, they have taught me that one of their greatest needs is to *confront the pain of their loss*. Poetry, traditionally an emotion-filled form, certainly helps them meet this need. "Emotions, now, are heated like a stew / My thoughts and feelings are astir in agony," says Raymond Rogers in *Empathy With Anguish*. In *Lonely Holidays,* Jeanne Losey embraces her Christmas grief: "How the holidays hurt when you're lonely / All that Christmas cheer cuts like a knife / I think I could sit in a corner / And just cry for the rest of my life."

Another critical and ongoing need for mourners is to *remember the person who died,* for it is in coming to peace with the past that we are able to live fully in the present and the future. Many of the poems in this book capture healing memories. Betty Simmons describes her deceased son's hands expressing their love for his children in her poem, *My Father's Hands:* "I still feel my father's hands / When I close my eyes at night / How they tucked me into bed / Before switching off the light."

Mourners have also taught me that they need to *search for the meaning of the life and death of the person who died* — and, by extension, the meaning of their own life and impending death. Poetry, as you'll see throughout this poignant collection, often helps mourners give voice to their search for meaning. "Life is like a butterfly / Softly, softly ... / One never knows why ... : writes

Geraldine Reeves. Mourner Peggy Kocisin arrives at a similar bittersweet conclusion in her poem *Dreams:* "I must dream new dreams / Make new promises / See new visions / Cherish new hopes / / But somehow they are not / As sweet as the old ones."

Mourners heal in grief by coming to a cognitive, emotional and spiritual place I call *reconciliation.* Reconciliation does not mean getting *over* grief, it means growing *through* it. With reconciliation, mourners feel a renewed sense of energy and confidence, an ability to fully acknowledge the reality of the death and the capacity to become reinvolved with the activities of living. They also come to acknowledge that pain and grief are difficult but necessary parts of living.

Many of the poets herein have achieved such reconciliation, and in sharing their healing lessons with us, they help us to heal, too. "Very slowly, I am learning there is room / For joy and fun and cherished moments with friends / In this hurry-up world ..." Beth Lorber teaches us in her poem, *Loss.*

The great 19th century English poet, Matthew Arnold, said that "genuine poetry is conceived and composed in the soul." No poetry springs from deeper in the soul than that born of grief; and so, in my estimation, no poetry is more genuine. Read and reread this moving collection and embrace the healing powers of poetry.

Introduction
By Andrea Gambill

Perhaps short of music itself, nothing seems to calm the tortured soul more than the heart-touching emotion contained in poems that give us glimpses of hope, new perspectives, new philosophies. Wonderful poetry is like fastening the soul to a helium balloon — free to soar and find release; free to discover new and more glorious horizons. Poems represent thoughts eloquently garbed in creative imagination.

Over the years, *Bereavement* magazine has been proud to present hundreds of poems written by the grieving who have crawled the road of pain and contained their sorrow in the eloquence of verse. Sharing the summations of their journeys has often been their most valued reward. To know they have offered healing and light to others who would follow in their footsteps has been their highest moment of achievement.

This collection of some of the best and most popular of the poetry that has appeared in *Bereavement* magazine is brought to you now in the hope that your heart will discover new light and hope. We have wrapped the words in soft images of graphic beauty and gentle format.

We encourage you to absorb these words into your own heart and share them with others, because it is in the linking of our souls that we find peace.

Angels of the Snow

By Joanetta Hendel
Indianapolis, Indiana

Snow angels live in splendor,
  In a land beyond all tears,
Where time and space do not exist,
  No sadness, pain, nor fear.

Held closely to the bosom
  Of all Everlasting Light,
Each cherub frolics happily,
  In fanciful delight.

I long to be within their midst,
  Where crystal majesty,
Gives way to charming images,
  Of winter fantasy.

Let me follow close behind,
  When I've lived out my days,
The path where angels of the snow,
  Live and love and play.

The Bud

Author Unknown

And the day came
When the risk
To remain
Tight in a bud

Was more painful
Than the risk
It took
To blossom.

My Father's Hands

By Betty Simmons
Brownwood, Texas

I still feel my father's hands
When I close my eyes at night,
How they tucked me into bed
Before switching off the light.

How he turned once more to give me
A final goodnight kiss
And his hands would gently touch
My cheek … Oh, how I miss

Those sweet moments in my life
When we were a family.
His rough hands were always soft
When he reached to comfort me.

When he took me for a walk,
He would hold my hand in his,
And I felt so safe and loved.
These are all the things I miss.

Dad left work to go to lunch
And he never did come back.
Because he was shot and killed
By a bitter maniac.

But he left a legacy
And a goal I hope to reach:
To be as good a parent, and
To practice what I preach.

I will always love him so,
And forever will be glad
That I had him for awhile…
Such a wonderful dad.

Who Am I?

By Carol Sharp
Springfield, Missouri

Who am I now that you're gone?
I've asked this question so many times it seems
But the answer's not available —
Not even in my dreams.

Who am I since you went away?
The days go by; time won't stand still.
I wish it would,
But it's against my will.

I feel as if I'm fighting
To keep my head above water.
It's horrible to go on without you ...
Never to hear you call me "Mother."

Who am I without you in my life?
Reminders of you everywhere I turn
Are supposed to comfort me,
But it's you for whom I yearn.

My body feels so empty,
And the void's so hard to bear.
I plead to have my son back;
I have so much more to share.

Who am I when I can't care for you any more?
I miss you at noon when we'd have lunch together.
That was our time to visit,
And nothing else seemed to matter.

My heart aches, because
I can't fix you those special dishes.
You always bragged on my cooking
And rewarded me with kisses.

This rocky road of grief
Has many ups and downs.
I'm trying to travel it, falling,
But still keeping above ground.

The road is long and treacherous.
I know it has to be,
Because deep love, joy and laughter
Are the legacies you gave to me.

With a future of despair, who am I?
I know who I am.
I am still your mother,
Your comrade and your friend.

You may be gone from me,
But our love continues on.
No one can take that from me,
It's there from dawn to setting sun.

I'll miss you and want you
All the rest of my life.
I am the lucky one,
God gave me a son named, Mike.

Second Spring

By Beth Myers
San Diego, California

The second spring is here; I thought I would be brave.
But when I see the yellow mustard
Splashed along the rolling hills beside the road
We used to take, I need you at my side.

Why did you have to go?
When every precious hour
I loved you so ... I loved you so ...
    I loved you so.

A meadowlark's nostalgic song colors the quiet air.
My heart springs wide in quick response.
I turn to see the kindred joy I know you feel.
But no one is at my side.

Why did you have to go?
When every breath I breathed,
I loved you so;
    I loved you so.

The apple tree's in bloom beside the house we made.
Where God gave so many precious hours.
Your strong and gentle presence permeates
Each lovely spot we shared, and in my heart I realize

You could not go, because
I love you so!

Little Boy Blue

By Eugene Field

The little toy dog is covered with dust,
But sturdy and staunch he stands;
And the little toy soldier is red with rust,
And his musket moulds in his hands.

Time was when the little toy dog was new,
And the soldier was passing fair;
And that was the time when our Little Boy Blue
Kissed them and put them there.

"Now don't you go till I come," he said,
"And don't you make any noise!"
So, toddling off to his trundle-bed,
He dreamt of the pretty toys;

And as he was dreaming, an angel song
Awakened our Little Boy Blue —
Oh! The years are many, the years are long,
But the little toy friends are true!

Aye, faithful to Little Boy Blue they stand,
Each in the same old place.
Awaiting the touch of a little hand,
The smile of a little face.

And they wonder,
as waiting the long years through
In the dust of that little chair,
What has become of our Little Boy Blue,
Since he kissed them and put them there.

Beyond Dream's Edge

by Debbi Dickinson
Naperville, Illinois

Three new children play tonight
In a land beyond dream's edge.
Instead of sand, they play with stardust,
Getting glitter sprinkles on their hands.

Instead of coloring books,
They color rainbows
For God to place in the sky,
His promise to us below.

Instead of jumping rope,
They jump strands of sunlight,
Braided strong by His might,
Forever shining bright.

Instead of riding bikes,
They spread their wings
And fly to distant stars,
As all the angels sing.

Instead of snow slopes,
They slide down moonbeams,
Iridescent glowing streams,
Landing in heavenly green.

Instead of bouncing on beds,
They bounce on clouds.
Their laughter echoes about,
Just beyond dream's edge.

Instead of TV,
They watch sunrises, sunsets,
And all that transpires in between,
Secure that God knows best.

We meet at night in prayer.
I quietly wait to see them there,
Golden haloes on their heads,
In a land beyond dream's edge.

Instead of playing ball,
They catch the stars
Before they fall,
Loving the wonder of it all.

Stephanie's Cotillion

By Linda Gillman
Murray, Utah

As one who was done too soon, she lingers,
Perhaps in the form of a deer,
Prancing over headstones
Like a prima ballerina.

With the swiftness of a shape shifter,
She transcends
And ascends,
Enticed by the brilliance.

Music swirls inside her mind,
drawing her to the Source.
She climbs a translucent stairway,
In a glistening gown,
To the cotillion of her life.

Flowers sing with colors vibrating her welcome.
Those who danced before, wait eagerly for her debut.
The music stops. A hush falls over the room.
"She is so young, so fair," they whisper
as she is introduced to her glory.

Her shimmering blond hair
Reflects benevolent light.
Her face is radiant
As she takes her place in eternity.

It's Still A Blessing

By Alma N. Malanyaon
Toledo, Ohio

For my son, Jonathan.

Lost in the sea of grief,
Pained by a tragedy uniquely mine,
Hope and meaning seem all gone.

Dark clouds hover each morning,
Speaking of the same heartaches and pains.
Struggling and questioning each passing day.

Hundreds of questions to God were asked,
Why God? Oh God, my son,
Whom I love so much!

Then somehow led by the spirit,
To pathways never trod before,
With renewed awareness of the breaking dawn.

Live one day at a time, they say.
For the journey is indeed long,
And filled with painful memories all along.

Mysteriously, in the secret of time,
Tears and smiles become one;
Pains and joys bring calm.

Shadows of hope taking form,
Strength and willingness to reckon,
To search and no longer to reason.

For somewhere beyond the obvious,
God's love abounds to bring
Peace and comfort, and stillness of heart.

To look at suffering with deeper understanding,
That my own and those of others,
In this world are purifying.

Greater realization of the shortness of life.
Life's so precious, life's so fragile,
Only in love will we find its true meaning.

Loving and giving, our reason for living.
In generously serving others,
We gain wisdom, strength, and healing.

Go on with your life, so to love and to care,
For there are thousands of others,
With whom you can share.

Truly in death, there is life.
Life for those who continue to make love
The very core of our human act.

When suffering begets such meaning,
It's time to be grateful;
For this is a blessing.

Inner Tempest Stilled

By Beenie Legato
Glendive, Montana

Sometimes I sense a little flutter.
Like a shadow swiftly slipping by.
Or I hear a silent, gentle murmur,
Like a soft whisper from the sky.

Sometimes, I hear you call my name,
Or clearly see your face before me.
And I feel that you are with me still.
Then peacefully ... I come to know

As I am thinking happy thoughts of you,
You, my son, are thinking of me too.
Loving memories fill my aching heart.
As dreaming dreams of what could be...

Or might have been, if you were here.
Until the piercing pain of losing you
Comes tumbling down on trembling fear.
And clearly once again I hear you say,

"But Mom ...
What if I had never been?
You could not then in
Love remember me."

Troubled Child

By Gretchen Wasson
Bethany, Oklahoma

I was so scared to tell them about you.
  I felt so ashamed …
You were a "troubled child,"
  Not "perfect" like all the rest.

Stories of children loved by everyone …
  Sons and daughters with such promising futures.
Even though you were not like them,
  You were my baby.

Even though you got into trouble and took drugs,
  I was always by your side.
Even though you spent time in jail,
  You could not have been loved more.

At times you were so frustrating
  And seemed all bad,
Then you would do something wonderful,
  And I knew you loved us.

I don't need to feel ashamed anymore.
  It didn't matter what you did or who you were.
You were my child,
  And you did not deserve to die.
      I love you,
      Mom

The Little Unicorn

By Peggy Kociscin
Albuquerque, New Mexico

There lived a little unicorn
(From when the earth was new),
His coat so white it glistened,
His eyes a sparkling blue.

In innocence and beauty,
He danced through woods and streams.
The animals danced with him,
His heart aglow with dreams.

He laughed and played with rainbows,
So happy all day through,
He loved to kiss the flowers
As their petals shone with dew.

He wandered through the meadows
In the moon's soft, silver light.
He loved to gaze at all the stars
That lightened up the night.

He listened to the music
Of the birds that graced the trees.
He frolicked with the butterflies
And raced the gentle breeze.

But, as he grew and learned of life,
The sparkle in his eye
Grew misty as he realized
Just what it means to cry.

He learned that there are shadows
In spite of shining sun.
The more he grew, he found that life
Was never **always** fun.

For now he'd learned of feelings
That come from deep within;
No longer in the "dream world"
Where (for so long) he'd been.

His gentle heart desired
But to know the pleasure of
To give and to receive
The very precious gift of love.

To love meant to be happy,
And yet it also brought him pain;
For those he loved could hurt him
Again ... and yet again.

His mother held him lovingly
And tried to ease his fears
About the sadness life could bring ...
The lonely, bitter tears.

She said, "Life is like a mountain,
(And surely this is true)
That we must climb as best we can.
There's no 'around' or 'through.'"

The unicorn tried tirelessly,
And gave the climb his best;
But he felt it was not good enough,
He felt he'd failed the test.

He could not understand it
When he felt himself rejected —
When all his gentle being asked
Was but to be accepted.

All this was just too much for him,
He knew not what to do.
That he was special as **himself,**
Somehow, he never knew.

His spirit crushed, he felt defeated,
And lonely tears would start.
Not understanding how to love,
It simply broke his heart.

But now he's in a loving place
Where all his pain has ceased,
Where all accept him and his love,
Where all he knows is peace.

A loving Being tells him,
"You're delightful as you are."
His spirit free, his brilliance now
Outshines the brightest star!

Hearts

By Forest R. Whatley
Jackson, Michigan

Hearts in grief must seek relief
   in memories and tears
Of what was shared with those who cared
   together all those years.

      Past heart's torn rift we seek to lift
         the hopes of those who stay
      On earthy soil and still must toil
         through long and bitter day.

For those who die, we wonder why
   the time for them is now,
Yet we must sorrow then face tomorrow
   and muddle through somehow.

      This is not the end, we'll meet again
         God's promise will be kept,
      But all the same, I feel no shame
         in all the tears I've wept.

With God's own grace, I'll see your face
   when it is my turn to die.
I loved you so, just that, no more;
   for now, I'll say goodbye.

A Lonely Stream

By Geraldine F. Reeves
Carmel, California

I sit beside a lonely stream,
It talks to me, invades my dream.
Rippling laughter over the rocks,
Precious stones of memory blocks.

Then it turns to melody,
Our love song 'haunts my reverie.'
A picnic 'neath a sky of blue,
Our first embrace when love was new.

Life was so sweet and tender then,
I wish we shared it once again.
And though my dreams may be in vain,
I love to hear that old refrain.

When I sit beside a lonely stream,
It talks to me, invades my dream.
Rippling laughter over the rocks,
Dear, sweet memories it soon unlocks.

Anger!

By Joanetta Hendel
Indianapolis, Indiana

Don't tell me that you understand,
  Don't tell me that you know.
Don't tell me that I will survive,
  How I will surely grow.

Don't tell me this is just a test,
  That I am truly blessed,
That I am chosen for this task,
  Apart from all the rest.

Don't come at me with answers
  That can only come from me,
Don't tell me how my grief will pass ...
  That I will soon be free.

Don't stand in pious judgment
  Of the bonds I must untie.
Don't tell me how to suffer,
  And don't tell me how to cry.

My life is filled with selfishness,
  My pain is all I see,
But I need you, and I need your love ...
  Unconditionally.

Accept me in my ups and downs,
  I need someone to share,
Just hold my hand and let me cry,
  And say, "My friend, I care."

Missing You

By Edna T. Burch
Westland, Michigan

Each loss is very different,
The pain is so severe.
Will I ever stop missing
This one I loved so dear?

Good times we had together,
The moments that we shared,
We didn't have to tell each other
How much we really cared.

I never dreamed you'd go away,
Never thought of sorrow.
So sure you'd always be here,
Took for granted each tomorrow.

Now my life is all confused
Since you went away.
You took a part of me
And for help I daily pray.

But when God sent you to me
He never said that you were mine,
That I could keep you always —
Only borrowed for a time.

Now, He's called you home,
I'm sad and I shed tears.
Yet I'm glad He loaned you to me
And we had these many years.

Others Who Have Gone Before

By Joanetta Hendel
Indianapolis, Indiana

Others who have gone before
Hold up my trembling hand.
They comfort me in the blind despair
I cannot understand.

They suffer with me when I hurt,
Weep with me in my pain,
Remind me that we are not lost …
Though I must now remain.

Those who've gone before me,
Hear me when I cry.
Sing softly with me soothing chords
Of unsung lullabies.

Mourn anniversaries never marked,
A future I cannot keep.
They gently kiss the pain away,
And love my heart to sleep.

The ones who've gone before me
Hold me in my dreams.
They gently stroke my furrowed brow,
And calm my silent screams.

They love me in my heartache,
Wait quietly nearby,
Hold patiently, one to another
Till I join them by and by.

Healing Dreams

By Colleen Burgess
St. Louis, Missouri

You touched my life the way no other heart could.
You brought a smile to my face and brightened my day.
My heart beats painfully over your absence,
And thoughts of you fill me with a bittersweet ache.

Not a day goes by that you are not on my mind.
I wonder what life would have been like if you were still here.
Even though I know you're in a far better place,
I ache for you and wish you would have survived somehow.

I look to God for the answers to all my questions.
I ask Him why He made you imperfect
  and why He took you from us.
When I think my heart is going to break in a million pieces,
I see you in my dreams at night.

When I sometimes dream of you at night,
I wonder if it is really you,
Reassuring me of your happiness,
Or just my mind, fulfilling my desperate wishes.

When I do have those precious dreams,
And I see your smiling face and sparkling eyes,
I know you have achieved a happiness and perfection
That no one alive could ever dream of achieving.

When I have those dreams, I stop grieving for a little while
And feel a reassuring peace inside my heart.
I know one day I will see you and be with you once again,
And it is easier to find the strength to get through the grief.

Do Not Stand at my Grave and Weep

By Mary E. Frye

Do not stand at my grave and weep,
  I am not there, I do not sleep.

I am a thousand winds that blow,
  I am the softly falling snow.
I am the gentle showers of rain,
  I am the fields of ripening grain.

I am in the morning hush,
  I am in the graceful rush
Of beautiful birds in circling flight.
  I am the star-shine of the night.

I am in the flowers that bloom,
  I am in a quiet room.
I am in the birds that sing,
  I am in each lovely thing.

Do not stand at my grave and cry,
    I am not there—
      I did not die.

The Home-Going

By Annette Lassahn
Farmville, Virginia

Home — such a beautiful-sounding word!
What pictures form in our hearts.
To some, the sight of a cottage small
In a quiet place apart,

Where souls can rest and be content
And each heart find sweet release.
Where the tensions of life can drain away,
Leaving only joy and peace.

To some, a stately mansion appears,
As in their mind's eye they see
A place of their own that's sheltered them
On life's rough and stormy sea.

It matters not home's size nor shape,
For whatever life may bring,
Our hearts feel secure within its walls,
And our souls with joy can sing.

But greater still is a Heav'nly home
Where from pain we'll be set free.
No heartaches or sorrow enter there
Throughout all eternity.

Now they have gone to that land of peace
Never again will they roam.
Can't you just feel their joy when He said
"Isn't it good to be Home?"!

Facing it Alone

By Mary E. Shaffer
Edwardsville, Illinois

They say, "But she is dead, my dear!" all those who were not there
To share a lonely vigil over all I had to bear.
Through days of unfamiliar halls and unfamiliar faces,
Struggling to hold onto hope in that strangest of all places.

But by and by, I found love there to bolster and support me
While the ravages of illness bore down on her so cruelly.
That body prone upon the bed, unrecognizable,
Was this my child who could not breathe, so distressed and miserable?

The eyes that never opened and the mouth that never tried
That completely quiet figure somehow yet was still alive.
With wires and tubes and frightful things, they strove to hold her life ...
How much was she aware of through long days and longer nights?

"Speak to her of courage,
Never fail to try!
Though you think she does not hear you,
(You must never dare to cry!)"

The days grew into weeks but improvement never came ...
It finally was apparent we were bound to lose the game.
At long last came those dreaded words, "Her heart will soon stop now.
Please try to say that you agree to let her go somehow."

With halting affirmation, I accepted this decree;
There was noting left to cling to ... I must lose a part of me!
Oh, for a chance that I could take her place and set her free
But such an opportunity just wasn't there for me.

28

The weeks between that sterile room and back to my narrow bed
Had now drawn to a close and my body felt like lead.
For I had held within my arms the reason for my life.
And offered her at last to God, resigned now to my plight.

But still the journey wasn't done there still was much to do.
A pink dress and spring flowers and soft things were her due.
"How brave you are, how strong!" I was met with salutations ...
(God only lends us what we need to face our tribulations.)

For grief is waiting in the wings, waiting for a cue
To move into your life and make a lasting change in you.
Indeed, why does God give us these sweet and lovely things
To grow and bloom and flourish and to make our hearts to sing?

When the monstrous and unspeakable sweeps down to lay them low,
And wreck and crush those bodies when we've learned to love them so.
"But she is dead," and now, "Put this behind you, dear."
However well intended, they're not words I want to hear.

Can we forget the darkness and remember just the light?
That's just what everyone will say but the story doesn't read that way.
How do I draw a veil over part of what has passed?
But surely will also shut out the things I want to last.

Yes, joys and smiles and happiness return to haunt again,
But grief has made them poignant which they never were back then.
But this alone I won't forget — and it is dear to me —
Three days before the end she raised her brows to answer me.

I held her face in both my hands and asked her if she knew
That I was there beside her, and was she happy for this, too?
The weakness of her quick response was all that she could give
And this is all she gave to me from that which in her lived.

You tell me, "She is dead, my dear," but that never will be true
For what is gone was just a shell that somehow her soul outgrew.
The beauty of her spirit dwells in my heart, alive;
And I hope within her children when I cease to survive.

Another swept away too soon leaving me in solitude.
Please don't say that they are "dead" while I still love them as I do.
They're quite alive to me! The other thought is there — in you.

Memories Of Love

Geraldine F. Reeves
Carmel, California

Precious love letters from long ago,
Neatly tied with a pale-blue bow.
Each one still saying, "I love you so!"
 Memories of love.

Yellow and faded, they e'er entwine
Joy in the heart like a valentine.
As in days gone by, they still define
 Memories of love.

Tarrying in the grip of the past
Is the magic of love and bonds that last.
A peek through the years, a looking glass.
 Memories of love.

Tenderness and pain give full measure
To lifelong love and all its treasure.
Sweet remembrance of sweeter pleasure.
 Memories of love.

Tho' the day came when we had to part,
These dear love letters will always start
Deep yearnings of love for my sweetheart.
 And memories of love.

The Angel On Your Shoulder

By Jackie Huston
Lena, Wisconsin

There's an angel on your shoulder
Though you may not know she's there,
She watches over you day and night
And keeps you in her care.

There's an angel on your shoulder
Watching you learn and grow
Keeping you safe from danger
And nurturing your soul.

She'll be there through your triumphs
She'll dance on clouds with pride,
She'll hold your hand through
    disappointments and fears,
Standing faithfully by your side.

In her lifetime this angel was strong and true,
And stood up for what was right.
In your life you'll be faced with decisions and trials
And she'll shine down her guiding light.

Life holds so much in store for you,
So remember as you grow older,
There are no heights you cannot reach
'Cause there's an angel on your shoulder.

Breakthrough

By Nel de Keijzer
Santa Barbara, California

The tears of grief
   Have washed away
      The clouds of sorrow,
         And vision now is clarified

I miss you still,
   But see you new
      In light of joy
         And smile at your remembrance.

The love we shared
   Still here to give
      And to experience
         The joy that comes from that, IS YOU!!

Love

By Nancy Ann Robinson
Stuart, Florida

How can I *BE* without you?

It's so much more than
the empty side of the bed.

It's so much worse than
no more private jokes.

It's no more rest or surety,
no silent strength upholding.

And what is worse, it's no one
to love or no one to love me.

It's more than loneliness,
this end of hope.

You are no more ...
forever, now, you are *was*.

You are yesterday's gift —
memories don't serve today.

Remembering is a sweet cage,
forgetting is another.

I am forced to *this* day, because
I live without your essence,

Because you died.

When Summer Fades

By Geraldine F. Reeves
Carmel, California

When summer fades into leaves of gold,
My heart listens for the still untold
Story of my love within my arms ...
Now gone forever, like summer's storms.

Soon blessed by snow and soft firelight
Warming hearts and dark, cold nights.
Sweeter dreams beside a fire
Stir my heart with one desire...

Remembered love,
When summer fades.

Empathy With Anguish

By Raymond F. Rogers
Greensboro, North Carolina

Don't tell me that you understand
The anguish stirring in my soul.
Like a pot about to boil and pop its cover,
I rock upon the range-top of events!

What can you understand? I do not understand myself.
Emotions, now, are heated like a stew.
My thoughts and feelings are astir in agony.
Which bubbles do you understand?

In this state, I do not care to hear about
the crosses we must bear.
Necessity has brought about my troubles;
I do not need reminding I must yield.
Right now I feel, and how I feel is quite enough!

Like a pot about to boil and pop its cover,
I rock upon the range-top of events!
You may hold me close, take the heat,
Rock with me, and share the horror,

But if you can't bear the horrifying truth;
Don't say you understand!

I See Her With Long, Dark Wisps

By Laurie Brace
Berkeley, California

I see her with long, dark wisps of hair
    Flowing in the breeze of life.
Blue eyes weeping to summon more time
    To run barefoot in the sands of time.

But she had to appease the goddesses,
    So they gently led her soul to the heavens,
There to reside with them
    Where the sands of time are endless.

Rise Up Slowly, Angel

by Diane Robertson
Foxboro, Massachusetts

Rise up slowly, Angel.
I cannot let you go.
Just drift softly 'midst the faces,
In sorrow now bent low.

Ease the searing anger,
Born in harsh, unyielding truth
That Death could steal my loved one
From the glowing blush of youth.

Rise up slowly, Angel.
Do not leave me here, alone,
Where the warmth of mortal essence
Lies replaced by cold, hard stone.

Speak to me in breezes,
Whispered through the drying leaves,
And caress my brow with raindrops
Filtered by the sheltering trees.

Rise up slowly, Angel,
For I cannot hear the song
Which calls you through the shadows
Into the light beyond.

Wrap me in a downy cape
Of sunshine, warm with love,
And kiss a tear-stained mother's face
With moonlight from above.

Then, wait for me at sunset,
Beside the lily pond,
And guide me safely homeward
To your world, which lies beyond.

Just spread your arms to take me
In reunion's sweet embrace,
And we shall soar, together,
To a different time and place.

To Lose A Loved One

By Joan Clayton
Portales, New Mexico

To lose a loved one is hard to bear.
So deep is all the sorrow.
The pain, the anguish, the loneliness,
And the great dread of tomorrow!

But the love, the memories and the joy
Death can never take away.
For they are ours to hold and keep
'Till we see that loved one again some day!

God will not leave us defenseless.
He said, "Your husband I'll be."
For He loves us more than life itself
And we are special, don't you see!

It's hard to understand this life.
We walk by faith and not by sight.
But know your loved one's with the Lord
And things will be all right!

Oh the bliss of that great day
When we reach that golden shore…
Meeting loved ones at Heaven's gate,
We will live forevermore!

That Jesus will comfort and soothe
Is my daily prayer so true,
Until the day He comes again
To take us to Heaven, too!

Colors

By Ramona F. Lyddon
Chester, California

See me RED with anger,
Out of control,
Life's unpredictableness shaking me.
How could he die?

I lash out at those who make life more difficult ...
Those on the other end of a business phone call,
Who don't understand,
Who make no effort to be kind.

Those who call, asking for his things,
Not out of memory, but out of greed.
How selfish and rude!
I scream the words ... silently.

Even cards can make me see red;
"I know you're strong," they say.
I know I am, but please, let me be weak.
Just for now, just for a moment.

See me GREEN, taking control.
My house will be in order.
The living room will be vacuumed and dusted.
The yard will be mowed, weeded and watered.

I laugh at myself, yet understand the need
    To be in control … and those around me?
        They are amused, I'm sure, but happy to oblige
        And plunge into the work, beside me.

See me BLUE, lonely, missing him.
    Needing him by my side, yearning for his presence.
        Heart aching with a pain unknown before,
            But now a constant companion … crushing pain,
                I can't breathe. I rub my chest to no avail; the pain
                remains.

See me PURPLE, in a sea of tears.
    Sobbing, the waves of despair roll in.
        The pain in my heart becomes knife-like.
        I think I cannot bear it another moment.
            Then, mercifully, the tide recedes.

See me YELLOW, calm, exhausted.
    The knowledge of the goodness
        Of our love flows into me.
I become aware that it is for eternity.
    The memories, special and precious,
        A treasure box of all we had, all we were together.

His words, forever imprinted in his journal, an on-going gift
    Telling me over and over again, of his love for me,
        His "sweet companion."

See me BLACK, in the darkness, I am alone.
  I am sinking into nothingness — a void.
    No one can go with me. Oh, it's so cold; it's so black.
      I cry out loud, "It's black, I'm cold."
        And, "Oh God, I'm afraid."

Arms hold me, and cradle me.
  A candle is lit, to bring me back to the light,
    To safety.

See me WHITE, without feeling.
  Too tired to feel, too overwhelmed to care anymore.
    If I care, and remember, the other colors will return.
      I don't have the energy to be touched by the colors.

Oh, the RAINBOW ... How it surrounds me
  Bringing an awareness of both the
    Heights and depths of joy and sorrow.

How I love the peaks, how I avoid the valleys.
  And, yet, the valley gives me a beautiful view of the peak.
    If I can only open my swollen eyes to see ...
      And bask in the glow of the colors.

My husband, Ted, died June 17, 1993

Hope

By Mary Dunn Jones
Tifton, Georgia

Hope is not pretending
That troubles will not come.
They come in time to all,
Though more appear to some.

Hope is the trust
That troubles won't last forever.
That with time and love,
Days will soon be better.

Hope is belief
That hurts will be healed,
As memories
In wounded hearts are sealed.

Hope is the faith
That there IS a source of strength,
That the love of God
Will provide the missing link.

Hope says that He will
Guide all the night through,
To the morning light
And refreshing dew.

To All Parents

By Edgar Guest

I'll lend you for a little time
A child of Mine, He said,
For you to love the while he lives
And mourn when he is dead.

It may be six or seven years,
Or twenty-two or three,
But will you, till I call him back,
Take care of him for Me?

He'll bring his charms to gladden you
And should his stay be brief,
You'll have his lovely memories
As solace for your grief.

I cannot promise he will stay
Since all from earth return,

But there are lessons taught down there
I want this child to learn.

I've looked the wide world over
In My search for teachers true,
And from the throngs that crowd life's lanes
I have selected you.

Now will you give him all your love   .
Nor think the labor vain,
Nor hate Me when I come to call
To take him back again?

I fancied that I heard them say
Dear Lord, Thy will be done.
For all the joy Thy child shall bring
The risk of grief we'll run.

We'll shelter him with tenderness,
We'll love him while we may,
And for the happiness we've known
Forever grateful stay.

But should the angels call for him
Much sooner than we'd planned,
We'll brave the bitter grief that comes
And try to understand.

Lonely Holidays

By Jeanne Losey
Shelbyville, Indiana

How the holidays hurt when you're lonely:
All that Christmas cheer cuts like a knife.
I think I could sit in a corner
And just cry for the rest of my life.

It's not fun putting up Christmas holly,
Colored lights, and the balls on the tree.
And the gifts, somehow, don't have much meaning
When you're not here to share them with me.

Since I don't want to spoil the kids' Christmas,
I will smile and I'll try to be brave,
But I wish I could skip this whole season,
And just go and sit by your grave.

For that's where all my thoughts will be, Darling.
I'll be there since you cannot be here.
On your grave I will place a poinsettia;
You will not be forgotten this year.

Silent Sorrow

In loving memory of my husband, LeVern, and son, Aaron.

By Barbara A. Holton
Charlotte Hall, Maryland

You left the house that morning so full of joy,
Just you and our two younger boys.
In the spirit of a moment, another driver's irresponsible decision
Took you both, and brought me silent sorrow.

Oh, how I cry each day just to hear your voice.
I ask God, "Why?," for I know this could not be His choice...
The two of you so full of life and energy to spare,
Was it time for you to go home to be in His care?

So little time has passed
Yet, the pain of grief grows stronger day by day.
No one can explain, no one can take away my pain.
Again and again I ask, "Why?," but I hear only silent sorrow.

I am told, "In time you will understand,
No need to ask why, because you will know His plan."
God has a plan, and time for us all to follow,
To depart our earthly journey and end our silent sorrow.

It's so sad to see you go, but because of our love,
Your patient, warm and loving spirits live on
In our hearts and give us strength to go on
In spite of the silent sorrow.

The Light

By Jeanne M. Roy
Pomona, California

You were there a moment ago
Or was it ages since we wed?
Now time moves on without you
And I hang on by a thread

Of my former self
Pretending to go on.
I'm caught inside a chess match
The Universe's pawn.

Oh, God, my mate!
The sharer of my soul!
How dare you break our sacred bond
And leave me less than whole?

Holding onto memories
That seem so precious few.
I'm afraid that I'll forget things.
Who'll tell me if they're true?

Do you hold me any longer?
Are you there, still standing by?
Please tell me how release goes.
What's my terror? Tell me why

This life must be so awful,
This suffering so prolonged.
Oh guide me now, my loving spouse,
Have I done something wrong?

To warrant such a punishment,
To have to stay, move on?
I wish I had the courage
To accept that you are gone.

And then, how I imagine it,
A wondrous peace descends,
Fills my soul with loving Light
And carries me, transcends

The hope of earthly union,
Yet something takes its part.
I'm moved by inner knowing —
The horse before the cart.

I'm placing Light before me,
I'm walking through the door.
The Pain, although it's listening,
Doesn't hold me anymore.

Unforgotten Dreams

By Peggy Kocisin
Albuquerque, New Mexico

Unfulfilled dreams lie unforgotten,
Broken, crushed by circumstances
That heedlessly, carelessly,
Shattered my life and my heart.

How I wish I could still
The wistful yearning
For those unrealized dreams,
The promises I made to myself

That once held the gleam and
Sparkle of expectation
And glistened
So hopefully in the sunlight.

Somehow, it just does not seem fair
That they now lie scattered,
Cruelly torn
Into a thousand pieces.

How sad it is to know
That any effort to recapture
And re-assemble them
Would be futile.

I must dream new dreams,
Make new promises,
See new visions,
Cherish new hopes.

But, somehow, they are not
As sweet as the old ones.

Life Is Like A Butterfly

By Geraldine F. Reeves
Carmel, California

Life is like a butterfly.
  Softly, softly ...
One never knows why ...
  It touches your cheek, then says, "goodbye."

Fragile and sweet, like blooming flowers
  Life's loves and trials last only the hours
That they touch your heart, then say "goodbye"
  Life is like a butterfly.

HOW?
By Henry Stephen Dewhurst
Falls Church, Virginia

How do I go on when all the love and life
I ever knew, or cared to know, is gone?
How am I supposed to look ahead
When I can't see beyond the tears?

Nor do I care what happens now to what is left of me.
How do I move beyond the dreams that we had yet to finish,
The hopes and plans we cherished so,
The castles in the air — still there?

How do I live with disbelief that jams my heart,
The pain that sears my very soul,
Relentlessly reminding me
That I am no longer whole?

Life goes on, I have been told,
But how do I?
How do I go on when all the love and life
I ever knew, or cared to know, is gone?

Life goes on and so do I,
Though never sure of how or why.
No longer are the yesterdays so wrapped in sorrows
Coming back as my tomorrows;

The rage is gone, the pain is less,
And I have cried all my tears.
The unrelenting reality
Has turned aside my disbelief,

And my shattered thoughts
Are healing now —
As much as memories will allow —
But still I know the weight of grief.

I search the shadows of my mind
To seek a peace I cannot find;
Each day is just another day,
Without a purpose to mark my way.

Without my beloved,
The brittle days and empty nights
Are little more than an endless sigh ...
But life goes on, and so do I.

Loss   By Beth Lorber Gassville, Arkansas

I am here among friends, smiling at their humor
And making plans for tomorrow.
But there is another person, lying curled in the corner,
Crying out in unbelievable pain.
>*That, too, is me.*

I am doing my household chores,
And the routine is familiar and satisfying,
A gesture toward a need for living.
But there is another person, lying in bed,
Willing her mind a blank, not wanting to think or be...
>*That, too, is me.*

I look at a lovely spring day,
A view of a world of growth and change,
A world only God could make.
But that other person stares through tears,
With unseeing eyes, knowing there is no God.
>*That, too, is me.*

I am surrounded by my family,
A gathering of love and joy and tenderness,
Of cherished moments and warm hugs.
But another person is there, whose arms and heart
Ache for one she can never hold and comfort.
>*That, too, is me.*

Very slowly, I am learning there is room
For joy and fun and cherished moments with friends.
In this hurry-up world, with no space or patience
For grieving, there may always be two of me,
And I'm doing the best I can for both.
>*That, too, is me.*

I Need to Be Heard

By Leslie Delp
New Freedom, Pennsylvania

I need to be heard …
Please don't tell me how **you** feel!

I need to be heard …
Please don't try to comfort me by
telling me, "You'll be better in time."

I need to be heard …
Please don't pacify me by trying to
"top it" with a hurt of your own.

I need to be heard …
Please don't look away when I mention
that precious name!

I need to be heard …
Can't there be anger among sadness
and misery?

I need to be heard …
Meet me where I am, and listen to me …

Until I don't need to be heard, anymore.

We Matter

By Joan M. Boyce
Millsboro, Delaware

Back then, grief held me in its bondage,
Its terrifying grip, unshakable.
Nothing mattered, nobody cared —
Not even me.

In that netherworld of existing,
Not dying, yet not living,
One day became another,
And still it mattered not.

Down, down, down,
I slid into that black hole of
Despair, despondency and depression,
And still it mattered not.

Family pressured, and were rejected.
Friendships died; anger, guilt
And self-pity raged on,
And still it mattered not.

Then one day was different,
Only the Lord knows why.
"Choose," He said, speaking within my heart;
"Life or Death," He said, "Choose — it matters!"

Turmoil reigned in my black hole.
Alone in fear and gut-wrenching loneliness,
Without self-confidence or self-esteem, I wavered.
"Who cares anyway," I said. "Not I, it matters not."

"Choose," He insisted,
As I trembled in the darkness.
"Choose," He said, "It matters."
Ever so slowly and painfully, an answer came.

"I choose Life,"
I said, with trepidation.
"I choose Life,
But I don't know how to live it."

"Make a step," He said.
"Reach out your hand,
"It will be taken," He said. "You matter."
And then He sent three ...

Three who offer their hands and hugs.
Who listen and share;
Who understand and love.
Three who matter.

Now there is light in the darkness,
Now there is hope in my heart.
Now the burden is lighter,
Now I am not alone.

We matter.

Threshold

By Fay Harden
Tuscaloosa, Alabama

Here,
spring comes suddenly
like a curtain of bright print fabric dropping from heaven,
transforming the land, shocking me.

Each year I feel I haven't been paying attention.
One morning I wake and my world is a festival,
gaudy with color, giddy ... like someone shook the champagne
and it spilled; its effervescence making the flowers early,
drunk and in love.

There is no memory of the neon leaves of autumn,
Winter's wind has pushed on. I'm glad it's gone,
it had become a guest who stayed too long,
a bore that drove me to my room.

Every year when the azaleas bloom,
I remember another spring.
That one wore a pall. The rain would not stop.

It poured into the open grave of my son,
It poured deep into my heart.
I was sure it would never, ever stop.

It did.
Though sometimes I wished it hadn't.
I was stuck between forgetting and remembering ...

Remembering won.
Now I see his face in the azaleas ...
They bloomed that spring while he died ...
I no longer hold it against them.

The Morning Star

By Gail Kittleson
Greene, Iowa

I am not like fake fireworks
   that blaze only on the Fourth of July,
     exploding with a bang
       against an unsuspecting summer sky.

I am not here for just a moment
   with a scintillating show,
     entertaining for awhile
       before I pack my bags and go.

I would not leave you
   with some sizzling starry dream,
     cascading past the night
       in effervescent, fading stream.

I am not like a fog that hides
   in winding slopes of land,
     I am the light that breaks it up
       as with an unseen hand.

I am the one lone star that
   watches through it all,
     and stays 'til early morning
       when the songbirds start to call.

I am the steady pulse of light
   when the bright day has ceased,
     giving those who see me
       unfathomable peace.

I am ... I am the faithful,
   unremitting Morning Star,
     and I will always be there with you —
       for I am where you are.

French Toast

By Fay Harden
Tuscaloosa, Alabama

I stand here before the stove.
All the ingredients are here,
The eggs, the milk,
Vanilla, cinnamon and sugar.

The frying pan is heating slowly,
Melting the butter,
And still I stand
In my robe and slippers.

I pick up an egg to break it in the bowl,
But I just can't do it.
I want so much to fix French toast,
Because my husband loves it so.

Just like my son did all his life …
Right up until he died.
I've lived this scene so many times since then,
Always with a tear and a sigh.

We'd had French toast at least once a week
For more years than I can remember.
How they ate! I'd laugh and complain,
Because I had to cook so much.

Once, in Florida, when we had French toast
For breakfast in a restaurant with friends,
He said, "This is okay,
But you ought to taste my mom's!"
I can still hear him saying it.

Now, I just can't do it.
I cannot cook French toast!

My husband never asks,
And while I stand before the stove and weep,
He pretends not to notice.
But I know he understands.
I just can't cook French toast.
Not yet.

Searching   By Susan Duggan Chicago, Illinois

For: Ambrose "Dugg" Duggan
Born into life November 29, 1921
Born into eternity January 10, 1993

Late night,
Wandering
From room to room
Searching for what?

Books on shelves,
Each in its' proper place.
Lined up and orderly
With nothing to say.

Family photos,
Framed and standing.
Memories to hold in my heart
Or flee in pain.

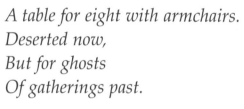

A bed with jumbo pillows
And cotton quilt,
Once so inviting of love and refreshing sleep.
I remember.

Drawers and little boxes
Holding far more junk
Than treasures.
Was it always so?

A table for eight with armchairs.
Deserted now,
But for ghosts
Of gatherings past.

Mirrors, small and large, lighted and magnified,
Combinations to see all sides.
I squint into these,
Checking to see who's there.

Unreliable mirrors all,
For I appear the same.
Late night wandering from room to room
This is what I find.

Memories of my Son

By Carol Sharp
Springfield, Missouri

Pictures of yesterday, happened upon,
Sweet, precious pictures of you, my son.
They're from a time that can't be erased,
And my heart fairly breaks as I gaze on your face.

Stirrings arouse in me ... words can't explain,
I want to go back, but I can never again.
Such a sweet, pleasant child, how I wish you were here.
To reassure me with hugs and your own special cheer.

To see that beautiful smile just one more time,
And hear that you love me, would make everything fine.
Though I yearn for all this, I know it can't be.
Oh God, why on earth did this happen to me?

The pain of losing you is so hard to bear,
I hurt so badly, does anyone care?
This is not what was supposed to be,
I want and need my son; can't you see?

I want to love him and care for him and have lots of fun.
And I'm sad, because those days will never come.
Instead, a precious life was cut short,
Twenty-two years of memories are my moral support.

I'm trying to live — day by day.
How can I do this? I wish it weren't this way.
This love for you is mine to keep;
Pain is the price for love so deep.

You're with me every day — you live in my heart,
And none of this will ever depart.
I'll look at your pictures, and remember with love,
Because you're at peace now ... with God above.

My Brief Rainbow

By Peggy Kociscin
Albuquerque, New Mexico

Rainbows appear only on dreary, rainy days.
They beautify the world for a few brief moments.
These moments, however, can be spectacular.
YOU were my brief rainbow.

You entered my life
And stayed for but a short while.
Nonetheless, the memories of those moments
When you blessed us with laughter and delight,

Joy and smiles, charm and beauty,
Gaiety and happiness,
Mischief and silliness, sunlight and moonbeams,
Giggles and love (ad infinitum)...

Made the deluge, the tears of pain and anger,
Helplessness and fear, insanity and agony,
Sadness and heartbreak, emptiness and loneliness
Bearable.

Rainbows, however brief,
Make the world a brighter, lovelier place.
How grateful I am that I had you,
My brief rainbow.

The Quilt

By Kevin Clark
West Valley City, Utah

I saw The Quilt today.

Each panel lay in soft silence
On a cold grave of concrete floor.
Modest, mute memorials to those taken.

I walked with friends, but stood alone
As the spirit of the room gently
Wrapped itself around me in welcome.

Bright bedding celebrated each life,
A stark contrast to the disease —
A two-toned beast of black death and anemic white.

Twenty lives torn for each name marked gone.
Embroidered voices held nothing back.
The seams reached out to mend the gap.

A voice recited the names laid before,
A grim backbeat to an inner dirge
Heard only by those who would listen.

The quiet enveloped those who walked there,
And maintained the serene dignity
Of the most plain panels.

Tears, smiles, a vague heartache,
Emotions pulled forth by the power,
Each took a piece of the pain.

Fear and prejudice held at the door,
Repelled by love sewn in cloth.
The hall became a shrine of safety and warmth.

I saw The Quilt today.
I was taken gently
Into the memories of each life.

The Quilt touched, soothed and warmed me.
I now wear it wrapped around my heart
As I step into the cold of night.

The Stepping Stones

By Barbara Williams
Fort Wayne, Indiana

Come, take my hand.
The road is long,
And we must
Travel by stepping stones.

> No, you're not alone;
> I'll go with you.
> I know the road well.
> I've been there.

> > Don't fear the darkness,
> > I'll be with you.
> > We must take one step at a time,
> > But remember, we have to stop awhile.

> > > It is a long way to the other side
> > > And there are many obstacles.
> > > We have many stones to cross, and
> > > Some are bigger than others.

Shock, denial and anger to start,
Then comes guilt, despair and loneliness.
It's a hard road to travel, but it must be done.
It's the only way to reach the other side.

> Come, slip your hand in mine.
> What? Oh, yes.
> It is strong.
> I've held many hands like yours.

> > Mine was once small and weak,
> > Like yours; because you see,
> > Once, I had to hold someone else's hand
> > In order to take the first step.

68

Oops, you stumbled!
Go ahead and cry.
Don't be ashamed, I understand.
Let's wait here awhile and get your breath.

When you're stronger, we'll go on ...
One step at a time ...
There's no need to hurry.
Say, it's nice to hear you laugh.

Yes, I agree, the memories
you shared are good.
Look, we're halfway there now;
I can see the other side.
It looks so warm and sunny.

Have you noticed?
We're nearing the last stone,
And you're standing alone!
And look at your hand ...

You've let go of mine.
We've reached the other side.
But wait, look back.
Someone is standing there.

He is alone and wants to
Cross the stepping stones.
I'd better go,
He needs my help.

What? Are you sure?
Why yes, go ahead. I'll wait.
You know the way,
You've been there.

Yes, I agree,
It's your turn, my friend.
To help someone else
Cross the stepping stones.

Borrowed Hope

By Eloise Cole
Scottsdale, Arizona

Lend me your hope for awhile,
I seem to have mislaid mine.

Lost and hopeless feelings accompany me daily.
Pain and confusion are my companions.
I know not where to turn.
Looking ahead to the future times
Does not bring forth images of renewed hope.
I see mirthless times, pain-filled days,
and more tragedy.

Lend me your hope for awhile,
I seem to have mislaid mine.

Hold my hand and hug me,
Listen to all my ramblings.
I need to unleash the pain and let it tumble out.
Recovery seems so far distant,
The road to healing a long and lonely one.

Stand by me. Offer me your presence,
Your ears and your love.
Acknowledge my pain, it is so real and ever present.
I am overwhelmed with sad and conflicting thoughts.

Lend me your hope for awhile.
A time will come when I will heal,
And I will lend my renewed hope to others.

**For a free, full-color catalog/brochure
describing all our products in detail, write to**

**BEREAVEMENT PUBLISHING, INC.
5125 N. Union Blvd., Suite 4
Colorado Springs, CO 80918**

or call our toll free number:
888-60-4-HOPE (4673)
or fax us at:
(719) 266-0012

You can also visit our website at
www.bereavementmag.com

Magazine Subscription & Product Order Form

BOOKLETS (choose any combination of titles)	QTY	PRICE	TOTAL
1100 *Special Introductory Sample (one copy of each booklet)*		$15.00	

1-25 = $2.00 ea.	26-99 = $1.50 ea.	100+ = 1.00 ea.

Fill in quantity next to booklet number and enter total at right.

1101 _____   1104 _____   1107 _____   1110 _____   1115 _____   1130 _____
1102 _____   1105 _____   1108 _____   1112 _____   1116 _____
1103 _____   1106 _____   1109 _____   1114 _____   1117 _____

CARDS (fill in quantity next to card number)	QTY	PRICE	TOTAL

Order any combination of cards in multiplies of ten. See inside front cover.

1201 _____   1208 _____   1211 _____   1214 _____
1203 _____   1209 _____   1212 _____   1215 _____
1207 _____   1210 _____   1213 _____   1216 _____
New! *Hospice card* 1250 _____

10 Cards for $12	60 Cards for $57
20 Cards for $23	70 Cards for $63
30 Cards for $33	80 Cards for $68
40 Cards for $42	90 Cards for $72
50 Cards for $50	100+ Cards for .75 each

BOOKS AND PRODUCTS AVAILABLE FROM BEREAVEMENT	QTY	PRICE	TOTAL
1150 *Sad Ain't Forever (Cartoon Book)*		$4.00	
1160 *Food for the Soul (Poetry Book)*		$9.95	
1305 *Grieving With Hope*		$9.95	
1310 *Healing the Bereaved Child*		$39.95	
1340 *Grief Expressed When a Mate Dies*		$19.95	
1360 *The Journey Through Grief*		$19.95	
1370 *Healing the Grieving Heart* (Caregivers)		$9.95	
1375 *Healing Your Grieving Heart* (Bereaved)		$9.95	
1380 *A Broken Heart Still Beats (After Your Child Dies)*		$24.95	
1630 *Bearœavement Bear* (with crystal tear)		$7.00	
1635 *Beverage Mug ("May Love Be What You Remember the Most")*		$7.00	
1640 *Light A Candle* (Single Title Music Cassette)		$5.00	
1650 *Grieving Angel Pin*		$3.00	
1685 *Picture Frame and Memory Candle* (set)		$14.00	
1690 *Little Miracles*		$5.00	
1695 *Memory Box*		$22.00	

Order Total	U. S. Shipping & Handling	Order Total	U. S. Shipping & Handling	
Up to $5.00 ....$2.00		$50.01 - $100.00 ....$7.50		***Line A*** Subtotal
$5.01 - $50.00 ....$5.00		$100.01 - $500.00 ....$10.00		➤ ***Line B*** (for above products ordered)
		$500.00 or more ....No Charge		Total U.S. Shipping & Handling
CALL FOR SHIPPING RATES OUTSIDE THE USA				

The following products do not require additional shipping charges	QTY	PRICE	TOTAL
MAGAZINE SUBSCRIPTIONS			

Domestic   ❏ 3-Issue $17   ❏ 1-year $32   ❏ 2-year $59
Foreign   ❏ 3-Issue $28   ❏ 1-year $45   ❏ 2-year $78 U.S. Funds

1350 *Compassion and Bereavement Audio Tape Series*		$69.95	
1665 *EternaLight™ "The Embrace"™'*		$289.00	
1670 *EternaLight™ "The Sanctuary"™'*		$579.00	
7500 *Information packet for Grief in the Workplace*		FREE	

Memorial Tributes
I prefer frame size: ❏#1405 (1), $10 ❏#1410 (2), $25 ❏#1415 (3), $40

Bereavement magazine offers a 100%
guarantee of satisfaction.

*If you are not completely satisfied, keep the first issue with our
compliments and write "cancel" on the invoice or request a full refund.*

Line C TOTAL products without shipping
TOTAL (ADD LINES A, B, C)

All products will be billed at current pricing

---

1. Ordered By: *Print or Type – Please Don't Abbreviate!*

Name _____
Organization *(if applicable)*_____
Street Address _____
City _____ State_____ Zip _____
Daytime Phone: *(required to process order)* _____
This address is: *(please check one)* ❏ Organization ❏ Home   *Please allow up to three weeks for delivery*

2. Ship To: *Fill Out ONLY If Different Than Above*

Name _____
Organization *(if applicable)*_____
Street Address _____
City _____ State_____ Zip _____
Daytime Phone: *(required to process order)* _____
This address is: *(please check one)* ❏ Organization ❏ Home   *Please allow up to three weeks for delivery*

3. Method of Payment

Make checks payable to:
Bereavement Publishing, Inc.
❏ Money Order ❏ Visa ❏ Mastercard

Credit Card #: _____
Exp. Date: _____
Signature: _____

4. Mail to:

Bereavement Publishing, Inc.
5125 N. Union Blvd., Suite 4
Colorado Springs, CO 80918

FOR FASTEST SERVICE:
CALL: (888) 60-4-HOPE (4673)
FAX: (719) 266-0012 • 8:30 AM - 4:30 PM MST

73